Muhammad Rasulullah: The Last Prophet

Dr. Abidullah Ghazi
Dr. Tasneema Ghazi

IQRA' International Educational Foundation

Part of a Comprehensive and Systematic Program of Islamic Studies

**A Textbook in the IQRA' Program of *Sirah*
Grade One**

Muhammad Rasulullah:
The Last Prophet Grade.1

Chief Program Editors

Dr. Abidullah Ghazi
(Ph.D., Study of Religion
Harvard University)

Dr. Tasneema Ghazi
(Ph.D., Curriculum-Reading
University of Minnesota)

Editing

Huseyin Abiva

Fadel Abdallah

Illustrations

Brad Cornelius

Design

Robinson Design

Aliuddin Khaja

Printed in Singapore
First Printing June 2005
Second Printing August 2008

IQRA' International Educational Foundation

**7450 Skokie Blvd., Skokie, IL 60077
Tel: 847-673-4072 Fax: 847-673-4095**

Website:www.iqra.org

Library of Congress Catalog Card Number 94-65596
ISBN # 1-56316-179-6

IQRA'S NOTE

As-Salamu 'Alaikum!

This textbook, *Muhammad Rasulullah: The Last Prophet,* has been written for First Grade students as part of IQRA's comprehensive and systematic program of Islamic Studies, a project that has been designed to be an integrated educational system facilitating the teaching of religious knowledge from a cross curricular perspective.

Muhammad Rasulullah: The Last Prophet (and its accompanying workbook) is part of IQRA's latest effort to revise and update its publications. This textbook has been written in language comprehendible for First Grade readers. It is hoped that children will be able to grasp the concepts introduced in each lesson and adopt its teachings into their everyday life.

Muhammad Rasulullah: The Last Prophet not only introduces major aspects of the life of the Messenger of Allah but it also familiarizes students with basic ethical themes such as relationships with the family members, neighbors and friends. Children are also introduced to the fundamental etiquettes of daily actions such as eating and sleeping.

It is recommended that the teachers use the accompanying workbook along with the textbook during class time. The workbook has been designed to provide pupils with important exercises in comprehension and to aid in the development of critical thinking skills.

We invite you to join hands with IQRA' in our efforts to provide quality educational material. Please send us your comments and suggestions. It will be only through our cooperation and interaction that we will be able to build a viable and professional program of education for the coming generations, *Inshallah!*

Chief Editors
October, 2004

About the Book

The following write up presents highlights on the features of the textbook.

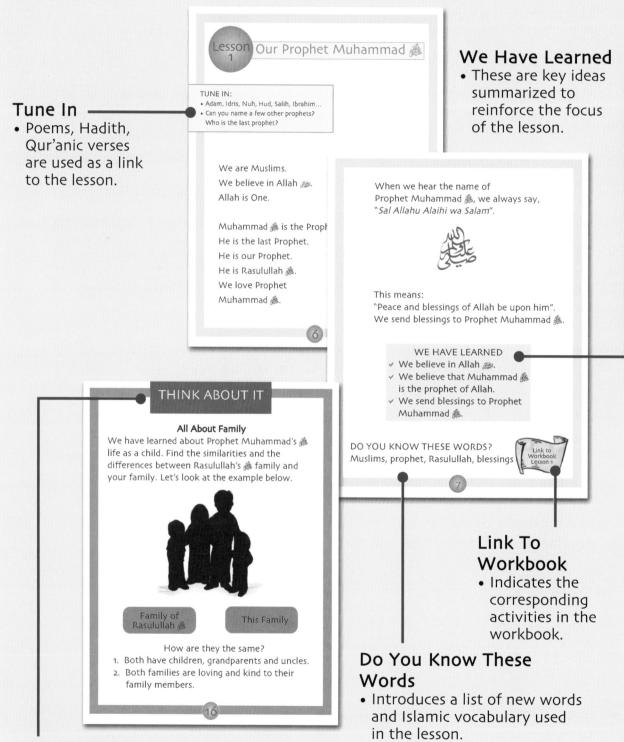

Tune In
- Poems, Hadith, Qur'anic verses are used as a link to the lesson.

We Have Learned
- These are key ideas summarized to reinforce the focus of the lesson.

Think About It
- Thinking skills are taught through the use of graphic representations.

Link To Workbook
- Indicates the corresponding activities in the workbook.

Do You Know These Words
- Introduces a list of new words and Islamic vocabulary used in the lesson.

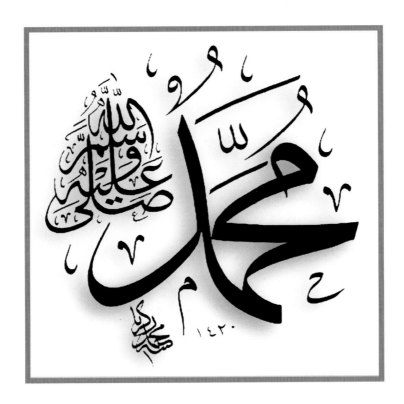

The publication of this book was made possible through a donation from the family of the late *Qazi Alauddin Ahmed* with the intention of Isal Ath-Thawab (إيصال الثواب) for him.

Please remember him and all the believers in your Du'a'.

Table of Contents

Lesson 1: Our Prophet Muhammad ﷺ . . . . .Page 2

Lesson 2: Makkah the Blessed City . . . . .Page 4

Lesson 3: The Family of Rasulullah ﷺ . . . . .Page 8

Lesson 4: Muhammad ﷺ Marries Khadijah ﵂ . . .Page 14

Lesson 5: Allah's ﷻ Message . . . . .Page 18

Lesson 6: Rasulullah ﷺ Teaches his People . . . . . .Page 21

Lesson 7: The People of Madinah . . . . .Page 26

Lesson 8: The Hijrah to Madinah . . . . .Page 30

Lesson 9: The Ansar of Madinah . . . . .Page 33

Lesson 10: Masjid an-Nabi . . . . .Page 38

Lesson 11: The Prophet's Favorite Foods . . . . .Page 41

Lesson 12: Rasulullah's ﷺ Clothes . . . . .Page 45

Lesson 13: Rasulullah ﷺ Comes back to Makkah . .Page 49

Lesson 14: Rasulullah ﷺ Passes Away . . . . .Page 56

Lesson 15: The Qur'an and Sunnah . . . . .Page 60

Table of Contents

Lesson 16: We Study the Qur'an . . . . .Page 63

Lesson 17: Our Masijd . . . . .Page 65

Lesson 18: We Pray Everyday . . . . .Page 69

Lesson 19: Praying in Jama'ah . . . . .Page 72

Lesson 20: As-Salamu 'Alaikum . . . . .Page 75

Lesson 21: Keeping Clean . . . . .Page 77

Lesson 22: Brushing our Teeth . . . . .Page 80

Lesson 23: Don't Get Angry . . . . .Page 82

Lesson 24: Eating our Food . . . . .Page 84

Lesson 25: Start With Bismillah! . . . . .Page 86

Lesson 26: Drinking Water . . . . .Page 88

Lesson 27: Love Your Mother! . . . . .Page 93

Lesson 28: A Good Friend . . . . .Page 97

Lesson 29: Helping Others . . . . .Page 99

Lesson 30: Karim and His Father . . . . .Page 101

TUNE IN:
- Adam, Idris, Nuh, Hud, Salih, Ibrahim…
- Can you name a few other prophets?
  Who is the last prophet?

We are Muslims.

We believe in Allah ﷻ.

Allah is One.

Muhammad ﷺ is the Prophet of Allah.

He is the last Prophet.

He is our Prophet.

He is Rasulullah ﷺ.

We love Rasulullah ﷺ.

When we hear the name of
Prophet Muhammad ﷺ, we always say,
"*Sal Allahu Alaihi wa Salam*".

This means:
"Peace and blessings of Allah be upon him".
We send blessings to Prophet Muhammad ﷺ.

WE HAVE LEARNED
- We believe in Allah ﷻ.
- We believe that Muhammad ﷺ is the prophet of Allah.
- We send blessings to Prophet Muhammad ﷺ.

DO YOU KNOW THESE WORDS?
Muslims, prophet, Rasulullah, blessings

Link to
Workbook
Lesson 1

TUNE IN:
- Which country/state do you live in?
- Can you find it on a map?

Prophet Muhammad ﷺ was born in Makkah. Makkah is a city in Arabia.

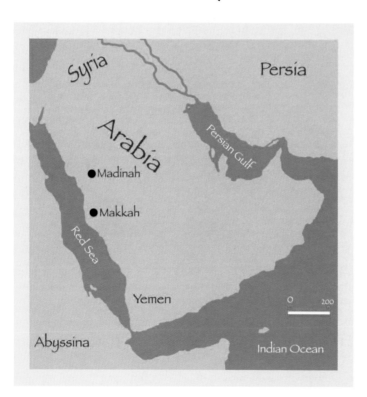

Look at the map.
Can you find Makkah?

Makkah is in a desert.
It is hot in Makkah.
In winter it gets a little cool.
Sometimes it rains there.

The Ka'bah is in Makkah.
The Ka'bah is the House of Allahﷻ.
We face the Ka'bah when we pray.
It is our Qiblah.

Muslims come to Makkah for the *Hajj*.

They come from the North.
They come from the South.
They come from the East.
They come from the West.

First they take a plane.
They fly to the city of Jeddah.
Jeddah is a big city near Makkah.
It has a big airport.

Then they take a bus to go to Makkah.
May Allah ﷻ help us to go to Makkah too!

WE HAVE LEARNED
- Prophet Muhammad ﷺ was born in Makkah.
- We go to Makkah for *Hajj.*
- The Ka'bah is in Makkah.

DO YOU KNOW THESE WORDS?
Arabia, Makkah, Ka'bah, Muslims

Link to Workbook Lesson 2

TUNE IN:

- Muharram, Safar, Rabi' ul-Awwal, Rabi' ul-Thani, Jumada al-Awwal, Jumada ul-Thani, Rajab, Sha'ban, Ramadan, Shawwal, Dhu'l Qada', Dhu'l Hijjah
- Do you know the names of the months in the Islamic calendar?

Prophet Muhammad ﷺ was born in Makkah.
He was born on a Monday.
It was 12th of *Rabi al-Awwal*.

رَبِيعُ الأَوَّل

His family was called Quraish.
His father's name was 'Abdullah.
His mother's name was Aminah.

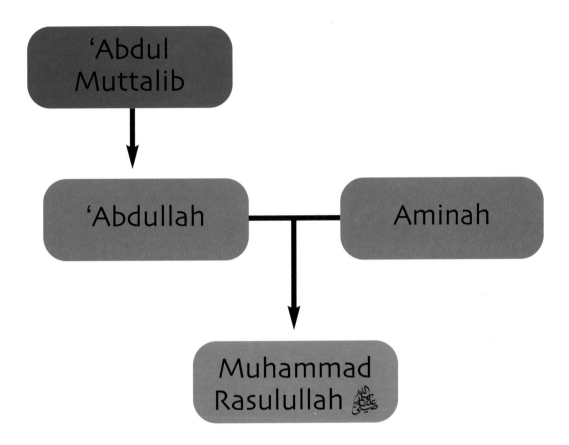

His grandfather's name was Abdul Muttalib.
Prophet Muhammad ﷺ lived with his grandfather
after his mother died.
Muhammad ﷺ loved his grandfather.
His grandfather loved him very much.

Muhammad ﷺ had many uncles.
One of them was named Abu Talib.
Muhammad ﷺ lived with Abu Talib
for a long time.
They used to go on business trips together.

Muhammad ﷺ always spoke the truth.
Muhammad ﷺ was an honest child.
Everyone loved him.

May Allah ﷻ bless Muhammad ﷺ!
When we hear his name, we say,

$$اَللّٰهُمَّ صَلِّ عَلَى سَيِّدِنا مُحَمَّدٍ$$

"O Allah! Send peace and blessings upon Muhammad."

WE HAVE LEARNED

- Muhammad's ﷺ father was Abdullah.
- His mother was Aminah.
- His grandfather was Abdul Muttalib.
- He lived with his uncle, Abu Talib, for a long time.
- He was always honest and truthful.

DO YOU KNOW THESE WORDS?
Grandfather, honest, truthful, trips

Link to Workbook Lesson 3

All About Family

We have learned about Prophet Muhammad's ﷺ life as a child. Find the similarities and the differences between Rasulullah's ﷺ family and your family. Let's look at the example below.

| Family of Rasulullah ﷺ | This Family |

How are they the same?

1. Both have children, grandparents and uncles.
2. Both families are loving and kind to their family members.

THINK ABOUT IT

How are they the same?
How are they different?

Rasulullah's family lived in Makkah.	PLACE	This family lives in Chicago.
Rasulullah ﷺ was an orphan.	FAMILY MEMBERS	These parents are alive.
Rasulullah's grandfather and his uncle took care of him	FAMILY RELATIONSHIPS	These parents take care of their children.

To be happy, family members must be loving and helpful to each other, just like the Prophet's ﷺ family.

Lesson 4

Muhammad ﷺ Marries Khadijah رضي الله عنها

TUNE IN:
- How did your father and mother meet?
- When did they get married?
- How many brothers and sisters do you have?

A very nice lady lived in Makkah.
Her name was Khadijah رضي الله عنها.

She was kind.
She helped everyone.
She had a business.

Muhammad ﷺ worked for her.
He worked hard.
She liked him.
She asked him to marry her.

Muhammad ﷺ said,
"Khadijah is kind.
She is nice.
I think I can marry her."

He asked his uncle.
Abu Talib said,
"Khadijah is a good lady.
She is a kind lady.
You can marry her."

Muhammad ﷺ was happy
He told Khadijah رضي الله عنها,
"I want to marry you."

Khadijah رضي الله عنها and Muhammad ﷺ
were married.
He loved her very much.
He was always kind to her.
They loved each other very much.

They were very happy.
They had six children.
They had four girls.

Zainab ﷺ

Umm Kulthum ﷺ

Ruqaiya ﷺ

Fatimah ﷺ

They had two boys.
But the boys died when they were babies.
Muhammad ﷺ and Khadijah ﷺ were sad.

Muhammad ﷺ and Khadijah ﷺ
loved their daughters.
They were good children.
They helped their mother.
They helped their father.

May Allah ﷺ bless them all!

WE HAVE LEARNED

- Khadijah ☙ was a kind businesswoman.
- Muhammad ﷺ and Khadijah ☙ got married.
- They had six children.
- They were kind to each other.

DO YOU KNOW THESE WORDS?
Business, marry, nice, love, kind

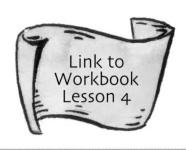

Link to
Workbook
Lesson 4

Allah's ﷾ Message

TUNE IN:

- Read, "In the Name of Allah who creates."
- Can you recite the first 5 *Ayahs* of *Surah Al-Alaq*?

Muhammad ﷺ wanted to know about Allah ﷾.
He wanted to know who made us.

He wanted to know who made the world.
He wanted to know who made the sun.
He wanted to know who made the moon.

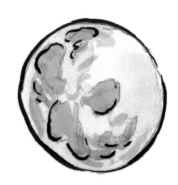

He went to a mountain.
The mountain was called Jabal an-Nur.
It is near Makkah.

Muhammad ﷺ found a cave. It is called Hira.
He prayed in the cave. He prayed to Allah ﷻ.

He used to stay there for a long time.
Khadijah ﵂ brought his food.

One day Allah ﷻ told Angel Jibril ﷺ
to visit the cave.
Allah ﷻ told Angel Jibril ﷺ to visit
Muhammad ﷺ.

Angel Jibril ﷺ came to the cave.
He asked Muhammad ﷺ to read.
But Muhammad ﷺ said, "I cannot read".

Angel Jibril ﷺ said, "Read in the name of Allah."
These are the first words of the Qur'an.

إِقْرَأْ

Allah ﷻ taught the Qur'an
to Muhammad ﷺ.
The Qur'an is the Book of Allah.
No one can change the Qur'an.

Muhammad ﷺ got the
Message of Allah.
He is Rasulullah ﷺ.
He is Allah's Messenger.

WE HAVE LEARNED
- Muhammad ﷺ prayed in the cave of Hira.
- Angel Jibril ﷺ asked him to read.
- Angel Jibril ﷺ brought Allah's Message.
- The Qur'an is the last message from Allah ﷻ.

DO YOU KNOW THESE WORDS?
Cave, Angel, Jibril ﷺ, message

Link to
Workbook
Lesson 5

Lesson 6 — Rasulullah ﷺ Teaches his People

TUNE IN:

"And you shall let them know that which has been ordained."

(15:94)

• Recite the *Shahadah* with your friends.

Allah ﷻ asked Rasulullah ﷺ to teach everyone the Qur'an.

One day Prophet Muhammad ﷺ asked his family and friends to come to his house. They all came.

He told them that,

"There is only one God, Allah
and I am His messenger."

He told them that:

Idols cannot be gods.
Allah ﷾ has made us all.
He has made everything.
He is the only God.

Many people became Muslims.
They believed in Allah ﷾.
They believed in Rasulullah ﷺ.

They all said,

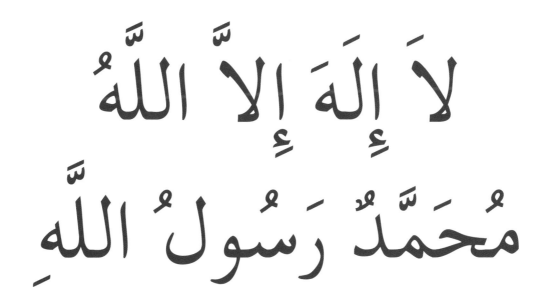

لَا إِلَهَ إِلَّا اللَّهُ
مُحَمَّدٌ رَسُولُ اللَّهِ

"There is no God but Allah, Muhammad is the Messenger of Allah"

But many people did not believe Rasulullah ﷺ.
They tried to hurt him.

They made all the Muslims live in a valley far away from everyone.

They had to live there for a long time. But Allah ﷻ took care of them.

WE HAVE LEARNED

- Allah asked Rasulullah ﷺ to invite people to Islam.
- Some people became Muslims.
- Those who did not, made the Muslims live alone in a valley.

DO YOU KNOW THESE WORDS?
Valley, idols, messenger

Link to Workbook Lesson 6

Let us talk about Islam

Prophet Muhammad ﷺ taught the people of Makkah about Islam. He told them that Allah ﷻ is One and that Muhammad ﷺ is Allah's Messenger.

Read and find out.

Allah ﷻ created everything.

Idols are not God.

Prophet Muhammad ﷺ talked about Islam

Prophet Muhammad ﷺ is Rasulullah.

Allah ﷻ is God.

All Muslim believe that Allah ﷻ is the One God and Muhammad ﷺ is the Messenger of Allah.

People from all over Arabia
visited Makkah all the time.

They came to see the Ka'bah.
But they did not believe in One God.
They prayed to idols.
They put idols inside the Ka'bah.

Rasulullah's family used to
take care of the Ka'bah.
They were called the Quraish.
Everyone knew them.

Rasulullah ﷺ went to the Ka'bah.
He talked to the people about Allah ﷻ.

He told them,
"These idols can't be gods.
They can't talk.
They can't do anything."

Madinah was a city far from Makkah.
One day some people from Madinah
came to Makkah.
They talked to Rasulullah ﷺ.
They liked what he told them.
They liked Rasulullah ﷺ.
They asked him to come to Madinah.
They asked him to live there.

Allah ﷻ told Rasulullah ﷺ and the Muslims to go and live in Madinah.

The Muslims were sad to leave Makkah. This move is called the *Hijrah*.

WE HAVE LEARNED

- People from all over Arabia visited the Ka'bah.
- People from Madinah invited the Muslims to live with them.
- *Hijrah* is the moving of Rasulullah ﷺ and the Muslims from Makkah to Madinah.

DO YOU KNOW THESE WORDS?
Move, visit, *Hijrah*

Link to
Workbook
Lesson 7

Lesson 8   The Hijrah to Madinah

TUNE IN:

- Let us sing this song,
  Tala' al-badru 'alaina
  Min thaniyyati-l-wada'. . .
- How did the Muslims of Madinah welcome Rasulullah ﷺ and the Muslims from Makkah?

All the Muslims went to Madinah. Allah ﷻ asked Rasulullah ﷺ to go to Madinah too.

The Kuffar of Makkah did not want Rasulullah ﷺ to leave. They stood around his house. They wanted to kill him.

In the night, Rasulullah ﷺ asked Ali ؓ to sleep in his bed. Then he got out from the back door.

Rasulullah ﷺ and Abu Bakr رضي الله عنه
rode fast camels.

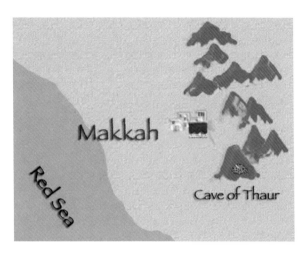

They came to a cave called Thaur.
They hid in the cave.

Some men came to look for them.
But they could not find Rasulullah ﷺ.

Rasulullah ﷺ and Abu Bakr رضي الله عنه came out.
They rode as fast as they could.
They stopped in a small town called Qubah.
Then they went to Madinah.

Every one in Madinah was waiting for them.
Finally Rasulullah ﷺ came.
The people were happy to see him.

They sang songs to welcome Rasulullah ﷺ.
They said, "We love you, Ya Rasulullah!"
"I love you too," said Rasulullah ﷺ.

Madinah became his home.
He lived there with other Muslims.

WE HAVE LEARNED

- Rasulullah ﷺ went to Madinah with Abu Bakr ﷺ.
- The people of Madinah were happy to see them.
- Rasulullah ﷺ and the Muslims lived in Madinah.

DO YOU KNOW THESE WORDS?
Ride, Qubah, hide, cave

Link to
Workbook
Lesson 8

TUNE IN:

- Rasulullah ﷺ said, "This is where I shall live. O Allah! Give peace to this place."
- Rasulullah ﷺ chose the home of Abu Ayyub al-Ansari ؓ to live in Madinah
- Can you guess why he called the Muslims of Madinah the Ansar?

Prophet Muhammad ﷺ came to Madinah.
The people of Madinah were very happy.

They loved Rasulullah ﷺ.
They loved the Muslims of Makkah.

They asked the Makkans to live with them.

The people of Madinah loved to share.
They shared their houses.
They shared their money.

They shared their food.
They shared everything they
had with Rasulullah ﷺ and the Muslims
of Makkah.

Rasulullah ﷺ and the Muslims of
Makkah loved the Muslims
of Madinah very much.

They called the Muslims of Madinah
their brothers and sisters.
Rasulullah ﷺ called them *Ansar*.
Ansar means "helpers".

Let us pray to Allah ﷻ.

"O, Allah! Help us to help others.
Help us to share with others.
Help us to help those, who need help."

"O, Allah! Help us to:
Help our neighbors.
Help our friends.
Help everyone."
Amin!

WE HAVE LEARNED

- Muslims of Madinah were called the *Ansar*.
- They shared everything with the *Muhajirun*.
- We should help everyone.

DO YOU KNOW THESE WORDS?
Ansar, Muhajirun, share

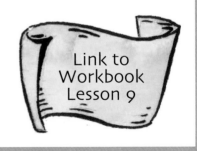

Link to
Workbook
Lesson 9

The *Ansar* were happy when Rasulullah ﷺ came.
They were happy with Muslims from Makkah.
The *Ansar* helped the people from Makkah.
Look at the ideas below.

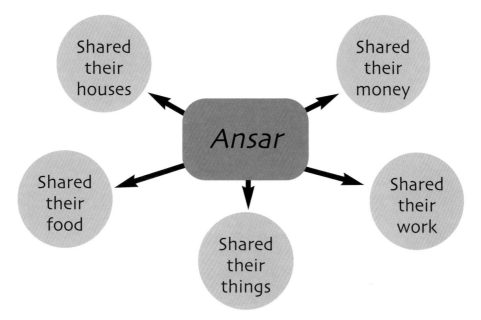

As Muslims, we must help others too, just like the *Ansar*. List how we can help others:

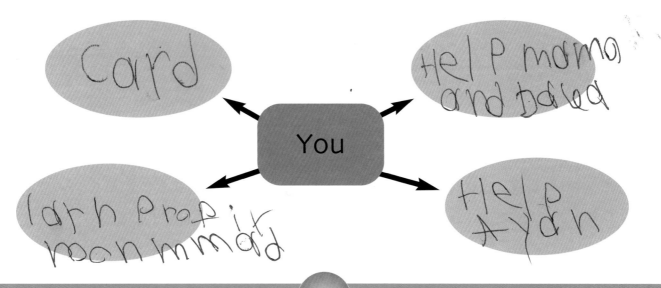

Masjid An-Nabi

TUNE IN:

- Rasulullah ﷺ said, "You will get one blessing for every step you take to the *Masjid*."

  (Sahih Muslim)

- What is the name of the *Masjid* that you have been to?

The Muslims of Makkah are called *Muhajirun*. The Muslims of Madinah are called *Ansar*.

Rasulullah ﷺ said, "Let us build a house of Allah in Madinah."

All the Muslims said, "Yes Rasulullah, we should build a *Masjid*."

Rasulullah ﷺ bought some land.
All the Muslims worked hard.
Rasulullah ﷺ worked very hard too.
They worked for many days.
Finally it was built.

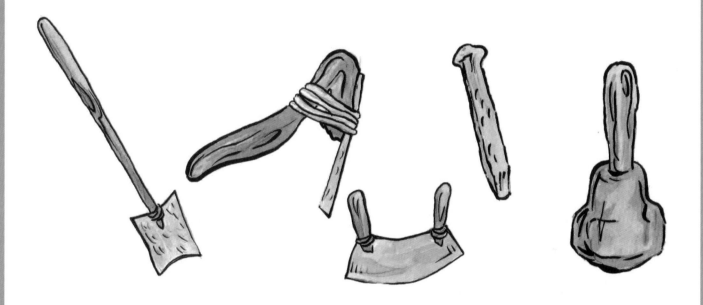

Everyone was happy.
They began to pray in the *Masjid*.
They prayed five times every day.

They called the place Masjid an-Nabi.
It means: the *Masjid* of the Prophet.

It now has a green dome.
It also has many Minarets.
It has Prophet Muhammad's ﷺ grave.
It is a very big *Masjid*.

We want to go to Madinah.
We want to pray in the Masjid An-Nabi.
We want to say *Salam* to Rasulullah ﷺ.
Let us try to visit Madinah.

WE HAVE LEARNED

- Rasulullah ﷺ and the Muslims built a *Masjid* in Madinah.
- The *Masjid* is called Masjid An-Nabi.
- Muslims want to pray in Masjid An-Nabi.

DO YOU KNOW THESE WORDS?
Muhajirun, Ansar, minaret, dome

Link to Workbook Lesson 10

The Prophet's ﷺ Favorite Foods

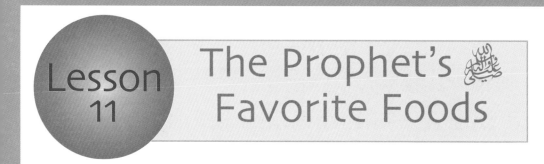

TUNE IN:
Meat, melons, beets, honey,
Milk, chocolates, pizzas, spaghetti
Favorite foods they are for me
Would you like some?
Come share with me
• What are some of your favorite foods?

Prophet Muhammad ﷺ did not have a lot of food.
He ate simple food.
He ate whatever was cooked for him.

He shared his food.
He told the cook that he liked the food.

He washed his hands before eating. Rasulullah ﷺ always said *Bismillah*. He said this *Du'a* before eating,

اَللَّهُمَّ بَارِكْ لَنَا فِيمَا رَزَقْتَنَا وَقِنَا عَذَابَ النَّارِ بِسْمِ اللَّهِ

"O Allah! Bless the food you have given us. And protect us from the Fire. In the Name of Allah."

He said this *Du'a* after eating:

اَلْحَمْدُ لِلَّهِ الَّذِي أَطْعَمْنَا وَسَقَانَا وَجَعَلَنَا مِنَ الْمُسْلِمِينَ

"Praise be to Allah, who fed us, gave us drink and made us Muslims."

He always cleaned his plate. He never wasted food.

Some of Rasulullah's ﷺ favorite foods were:

Dates

Bread

Meat

Honey

Cucumbers

Milk

Here are some more of his favorite foods:

Watermelon

Olives

Beets

Pumpkin

WE HAVE LEARNED
- Rasulullah ﷺ liked simple food.
- He always cleaned his plate.
- He said *Du'a* before and after eating.

DO YOU KNOW THESE WORDS?
Favorite, simple, *Du'a, Bismillah*

Link to
Workbook
Lesson 11

Rasulullah's ﷺ Clothes

TUNE IN:

Believing is *Iman*

To be clean is *Iman*

- Do you wear clean clothes?
- What kinds of clothes do you wear?

Rasulullah ﷺ liked to wear simple clothes.

He wore clean clothes.

He washed his clothes himself.

He always brushed his teeth.
He brushed his teeth with a Miswak.

He always kept his *Wudu*.
He always kept his nails clean.

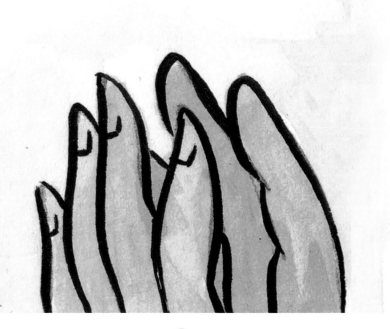

He always kept his hair combed.
He always washed his hair.

He liked to keep his feet clean.
He always wore his slippers.

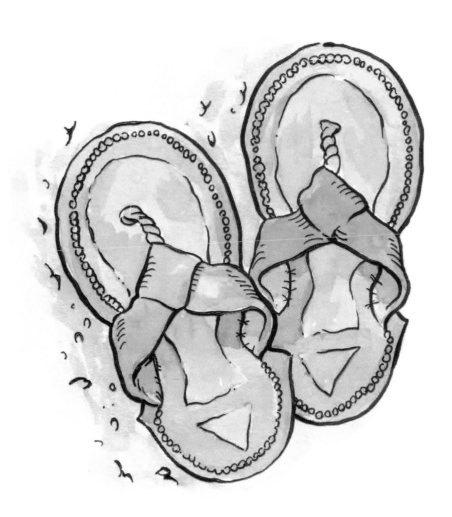

He liked to wear white clothes.
His favorite color was white.

And his second favorite color was green.
What is your favorite color?

DO YOU KNOW THESE WORDS?
Simple, clean, slippers, *Miswak*, nails

Link to
Workbook
Lesson 12

TUNE IN:

Hajj to Makkah,
At least once in our life,
We try to perform,
For the sake of our love to Allah.

• Rasulullah ﷺ and the Muslims left Makkah to live in Madinah.

• Do you think they would see the Ka'bah again?

Rasulullah ﷺ stayed in Madinah.
He could not go to Makkah for many years.
He wanted to go to Makkah.
He wanted to make *Hajj.*

The Muslims of Madinah wanted to go with him.
They wanted to do *Hajj* too.

Rasulullah ﷺ prayed to Allah ﷻ.
The Muslims prayed to Allah ﷻ.
Allah ﷻ said they could go.
Allah ﷻ told Rasulullah ﷺ
"All of you can go for *Hajj* now."

They left for Makkah.
Some rode the camels.
Some walked.

The Muslims stopped near Makkah.
They washed themselves.
They put the *Ihram*.
They prayed two *Raka't*.

They got ready for *Hajj*
Rasulullah ﷺ said,

لَبَّيْكَ اللَّهُمَّ لَبَّيْكَ

"O Allah! We are coming!"
Everyone said it after Rasulullah ﷺ.
Rasulullah ﷺ and the Muslims finally
came to Makkah.
He entered the Ka'bah.

The Muslims went around the Ka'bah
seven times.
This is called the *Tawwaf*.
They all did their *Salat*.
They all thanked Allah ﷻ.

53

Rasulullah ﷺ made the *Hajj*.
All the Muslims of Makkah were there.
All the Muslims of Madinah were there.

Muslims from many lands were there.
They were together in *Hajj*.

They heard Rasulullah ﷺ give
his last *Khutbah*.

He told the Muslims,
"Islam is the *Din* of Allah.
We are brothers and sisters.

Men should be kind to women.
We should follow the Qur'an.
We should follow Allah's Messenger."

إِسْلَامٌ

After the *Hajj,* Rasulullah ﷺ
went back to Madinah.
The Muslims went back to Madinah
with him.

They all thanked Allah ﷻ.
They were happy to do *Hajj* with
Rasulullah ﷺ.

WE HAVE LEARNED
- Rasulullah ﷺ and the Muslims went for *Hajj.*
- Rasulullah ﷺ said that all people are equal.
- We should follow Rasulullah ﷺ.

DO YOU KNOW THESE WORDS?
Ihram, Tawwaf, travel,
Khutbah, Din, Sunnah

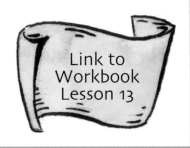
Link to
Workbook
Lesson 13

On to Makkah

Rasulullah ﷺ and the Muslims went to Makkah to make *Hajj*. Muslims in America make the *Hajj* too. Let us find out how the people went to Makkah then and now.

How are they the same?

Muslims during the time of Rasulullah ﷺ	Muslims in America Now
1. They went to the City of _____ for *Hajj*.	1. They go to the City of _____ for *Hajj*.
2. They wore _____.	2. They wear _____.
3. They all gathered at the _____.	3. They all gather at the _____.
4. They went around the Ka'bah ___ ___.	4. They go around the Ka'bah __ ___.

THINK ABOUT IT

Muslims during the time of Rasulullah ﷺ		Muslims in America Now
1. _____	**Transportation**	1. _____
2. _____	**Language(s)**	2. _____
3. _____	**Food & Drink**	3. _____

Lesson 14 — Rasulullah ﷺ Passes Away

TUNE IN:

"Inna lillahi wa ina ilayhi raji'un"

- When do we say this *du'a*?
- Do you know what this *du'a* means?

After making *Hajj* Rasulullah ﷺ came back to Madinah.

He was happy.

Everyone was happy.

One day he felt sick.
He got even sicker.
He could not even go to
the *Masjid* anymore.

Everyone prayed to Allah ﷻ.
They prayed for Rasulullah ﷺ
to get better.

But Allah ﷻ wanted Rasulullah ﷺ
to go back to Him.
Rasulullah's ﷺ work was done.

He taught people how to pray.
He taught people how to read the Qur'an.
He taught people how to be good.

He asked his friend Abu Bakr ﷺ to
lead the prayers.

Prophet Muhammad ﷺ passed away
in Madinah.
It was a Monday.
He was 63 years old.

Everyone was sad.
Everyone missed Rasulullah ﷺ.

WE HAVE LEARNED
- Rasulullah ﷺ became sick after *Hajj.*
- Abu Bakr ﷺ led the prayers.
- Rasulullah ﷺ passed away.
- Muslims have the Qur'an and the *Sunnah* to follow.

DO YOU KNOW THESE WORDS?
Returned, sick, sad, passed away

Link to
Workbook
Lesson 14

Lesson 15 — The Qur'an and *Sunnah*

TUNE IN:

Allah ﷻ says,

"That which is allowed by the Messenger, you may do. That which is not allowed, stop doing."

(Al-Hashr:7)

- Do you know what a *Hadith* is?

Prophet Muhammad ﷺ said,
"Read the Qur'an.
Follow the Qur'an".

The Qur'an is the Word of Allah.
Allah ﷻ sent it to Rasulullah ﷺ.
Then Rasulullah ﷺ read it to everyone.

We read the *Hadiths*.
Hadiths are the words of Rasulullah ﷺ.
We follow the *Hadiths*.
We do what Rasulullah ﷺ told us to do.

We follow the *Sunnah*.
The *Sunnah* is everything Rasulullah ﷺ did.

Rasulullah ﷺ left us the Qur'an.
He left us his *Hadiths*.
He left us his *Sunnah*.

Let us follow the Qur'an.
Let us read *Hadiths*.
Let us follow the *Sunnah*.

We read the Qur'an.
We act upon his *Sunnah* and *Hadith*.
We share them with our friends.
We share them with our brothers and sisters.

We take good care of the Qur'an and the *Hadiths*.

WE HAVE LEARNED

- The Qur'an is the word of Allah ﷾.
- The *Hadiths* are the words of Rasulullah ﷺ.
- The *Sunnah* is the actions of Rasulullah ﷺ.
- We follow the Qur'an and the *Sunnah*.

DO YOU KNOW THESE WORDS?
Hadith, Sunnah, action

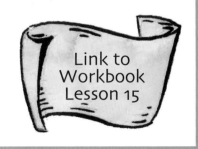

Link to Workbook Lesson 15

Lesson 16 — We Study the Qur'an

TUNE IN:
When we read
the Qur'an everyday.
Clean and bright
our hearts will stay.
• Do you read the Qur'an everyday?

The Qur'an is the Book of Allah.
Allah ﷻ wants us to read the Qur'an.
Allah ﷻ wants us to follow the Qur'an.

Prophet Muhammad ﷺ said,
"If you read the Qur'an
and share it with others,
you are the best person."

Let us learn to read the Qur'an in Arabic.
Let us learn its meanings and follow
what it says.

When we know the Qur'an well,
we should teach it to others.
We should share the Qur'an.

WE HAVE LEARNED
- Qur'an is the Book of Allah ﷻ
- We should learn to read the
  Qur'an and share it with others.

DO YOU KNOW THESE WORDS?
Learn, read, share, teach, best

Link to
Workbook
Lesson 16

Lesson 17   Our *Masjid*

TUNE IN:

Rasulullah ﷺ said,

"Whoever builds a *Masjid* for Allah
Allah will build a place for him in *Jannah*".

- Let us work hard to have a home in *Jannah*.

Masjid is the House of Allah ﷻ.
We pray in the *Masjid*.
We read Qur'an in the *Masjid*.
We meet everyone in the *Masjid*.

Let us help to build a *Masjid*.
Let us give our money.
Let us give our time
and build many *Masajid*.

Rasulullah ﷺ said,

مَنْ بَنَى مَسْجِدًا يَبْتَغِي بِهِ وَجْهَ اللَّهِ ،
بَنَى اللَّهُ لَهُ مِثْلَهُ فِي الْجَنَّةِ

"Whoever builds a *Masjid* for Allah,
Allah will build a place for him in *Jannah*".

This is Karim.
His sister is Selma.
They live with their parents.

Karim and Selma love their *Masjid*.

They keep it clean.
They help plant flowers.
The *Masjid* has a beautiful garden.

Their father built a shoe rack for people.
They helped their father.

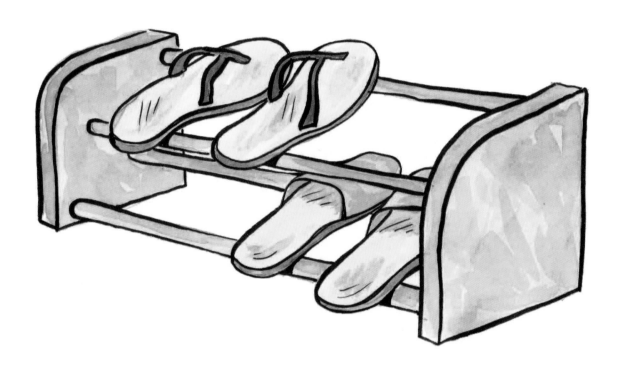

Karim and Selma always put money in the donation jar.

May Allah ﷻ be happy with Karim and Selma.
May Allah ﷻ help us to be like them.
May Allah ﷻ help us to build a *Masjid*.
May Allah ﷻ help us to keep it clean.

WE HAVE LEARNED

- *Masjid* is the House of Allah ﷻ.
- We should help build new *Masajid*.
- We should help keep our *Masjid* neat and clean.

DO YOU KNOW THESE WORDS?
Masjid, clean, builds, help

Link to Workbook Lesson 17

Lesson 18 — We Pray Everyday

Rasulullah ﷺ said,
"*Salah* is the pillar of Islam."

اَلصَّلَاةُ عِمَادُالدِّينِ

We pray every day.
We pray five times a day.

فَجْر We pray in the morning.

ظُهْر We pray at noon.

عَصْر We pray in the afternoon.

مَغْرِب

We pray in the evening.

عِشَاء

Then we pray at night.

Allah ﷻ wants us to pray on time.
He wants us to pray five times a
day, everyday.
Let us always pray five times a day.

WE HAVE LEARNED
- We pray five times a day every day.
- We pray in the morning, at noon, in the afternoon, in the evening and at night.

DO YOU KNOW THESE WORDS?
pray, pillar, noon, evening

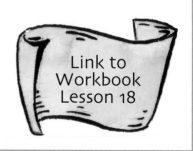
Link to
Workbook
Lesson 18

72

SALAH

We know that Rasulullah ﷺ loves *Salah*.
We pray five times a day everyday.
We can pray at home or in a *Masjid*.

How are they the same?

When We Pray at the Masjid		When We Pray at home
Fajr _____ Zuhr _____ Asr _____ Maghrib _____ Isha _____	Number of Fard Rak'ah for each prayer	Fajr _____ Zuhr _____ Asr _____ Maghrib _____ Isha _____

How are they different?

When We Pray at the Masjid		When We Pray at home
Pray with other Muslims. Special place only for prayer	Prayer alone or with other Muslims Place for prayer	Pray alone or with our family and friends. Any room in the house.

We pray five times a day. We can make our *Salah* at home or in a *Masjid*. But the best place is the *Masjid* because it is Allah's house.

TUNE IN:
Allah wants us to make *Salah*,
Five times a day *Salah* we offer,
And if together we *Salah*,
That's more reward together!
• How many times have you done your *Salah* with your family or friends?

We pray five times a day.
We can pray alone.
We can also pray together.
Praying with others is called *Jama'ah*.
Jama'ah means together.

Prophet Muhammad ﷺ said,

عَلَيْكُمْ بِالْجَمَاعَةِ

"Be in *Jama'ah*"

It is better to pray with others.
It is better to pray in a *Masjid*.
This is better than praying alone.
Let us try to pray in *Jama'ah*.
Insha' Allah.

WE HAVE LEARNED

- Rasulullah ﷺ has said that praying in *Jama'ah* is better than praying alone.
- We should try to pray in *Jama'ah*.

DO YOU KNOW THESE WORDS?
Salah, Jama'ah, try, reward

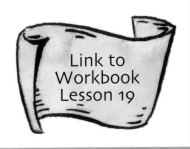

Link to Workbook Lesson 19

Let us pray.
We pray five times a day.
We can pray alone.
We can pray together.
Rasulullah ﷺ told us to pray in *Jama'ah*.

Salah Alone

Salah in *Jama'ah*

How are they the same?
1. Both are done for Allah ﷻ.
2. Both are done in clean places.

How are they different?

	SALAH ALONE	SALAH in JAMA'AH
RULES	There is no *Imam*	There is an *Imam*
NUMBER OF PERSONS	One Person	Two or more persons
REWARD	1 reward	27 more rewards

We all must pray. We must try our best to make *Salah* in *Jama'ah*.

Lesson 20 — As-Salamu 'Alaikum!

TUNE IN:
When we meet a Muslim
we say *Salam*.
"Assalam u Alaikum"
"Wa Alaikum Assalam"

We are Muslims, *al-Hamdulillah*.
When we meet each other, we say,
"*As-salamu 'Alaikum*."
"Peace of Allah be with you!"

اَلسَّلاَمُ عَلَيْكُمْ

When some one says, "*As-salamu `Alaikum*"
We say "*Wa `Alaikum As-salam*".
This means, "And peace of Allah be with
you too."

وَعَلَيْكُمُ السَّلاَمُ

Rasulullah ﷺ said,
"Say 'As-salamu Alaikum' before you talk."

He ﷺ also said,

أَفْشُوا السَّلاَمُ بَيْنَكُمْ

"Greet each other with *Salam*."

WE HAVE LEARNED
- We should say "*As-salamu `Alaikum*" when we meet a Muslim.
- In reply, we say "*Wa `Alaikum As-salam*".
- It means "peace be with you."

DO YOU KNOW THESE WORDS?
Peace, meet, *As-salamu `Alaikum*

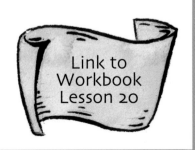
Link to Workbook Lesson 20

Lesson 21

Keeping Clean

TUNE IN:
- Allah ﷻ loves those who are always clean. Being clean is part of *Iman*.
- How do you keep yourself and the places around you clean at all times?

Aliya is a Muslim girl.
She lives with her family
in a little house.
She goes to school every day.

She takes a bath.
She brushes her teeth.
She combs her hair.
She wears clean clothes.

Aliya keeps her house clean.
She cleans the floor.
She makes her bed.
She throws out the garbage.

Prophet Muhammad ﷺ said,

"Cleanliness is part of One's Faith."

We should keep our home and *Masjid* clean.
We should keep our car and school clean.

WE HAVE LEARNED
- Muslims should always keep clean.
- Cleanliness is part of *Iman*

DO YOU KNOW THESE WORDS?
Cleanliness, *Iman*, garbage, teeth

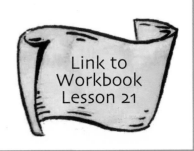

Link to
Workbook
Lesson 21

Keeping Clean

Muslims must be clean at all times. We must keep our bodies clean. We must keep our house clean. We empty garbage to keep our house clean. Some garbage is useful and some is not. We can reuse useful garbage by recycling it. Recycling means to use again. Can you name garbage that can be recycled?

Recycle	Can't Recycle
Plastic bags	Leftover food

_____ _____

_____ _____

_____ _____

_____ _____

TUNE IN:
- How do you clean your teeth?
- How many times a day do you brush your teeth?

Rasulullah ﷺ said,
"We should brush our teeth."

We should brush them every day.
We should brush them in the morning.
We should brush them before we go to bed.

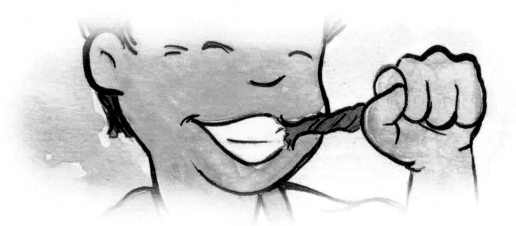

We should clean our mouth after we eat.
We should brush our teeth.
We should wash our mouth.

Rasulullah ﷺ said,

اَلسِّوَاكُ مَطْهَرَةٌ لِلْفَمِ مَرْضَاةٌ لِلرَّبِّ

"Brushing your teeth makes your mouth clean
and it makes Allah happy."

WE HAVE LEARNED

- We should brush our teeth everyday.
- Rasulullah ﷺ said that brushing our teeth makes our mouth clean and it makes Allah ﷻ happy.

DO YOU KNOW THESE WORDS?
Teeth, brush, wash, mouth

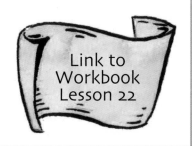
Link to
Workbook
Lesson 22

TUNE IN:
HEAVEN WILL BE YOURS
La taghdab walakal jannah.
La taghdab walakal jannah.
Don't be angry and heaven will be yours.
Don't be angry and heaven will be yours.

Rasulullah ﷺ said,

إِذَا غَضِبْتَ فَاسْكُتْ

"When you feel angry, keep silent."

Every one feels angry at times.
We cannot think when we are angry.
We may shout at others.
We may say bad words.
We may stamp our feet.
We may hurt ourselves.
We may hurt someone else.

When we are angry,
we should keep quiet.
We can drink some water.

We pray to Allah ﷻ to help us
and keep Shaitan away from us.

WE HAVE LEARNED

- If we are angry we should keep quiet.
- We sit down and drink some water.
- We should pray to Allah ﷻ to help us.

DO YOU KNOW THESE WORDS?
Anger, shout, silent

Link to
Workbook
Lesson 23

Lesson 24 — Eating our Food

TUNE IN:
- Share with your friends some good eating habits that you practice at home.
- What good eating habits of Rasulullah ﷺ do you know?

Allah ﷻ has made us.
He gives us food to eat.
He gives us water to drink.
He gives us air to breathe.

We should do *Wudu*
before we eat.
We should do *Wudu*
after we eat too.
Allah ﷻ is happy with
us when we do this.

Prophet Muhammad ﷺ said,

بَرَكَةُ الطَّعَامِ الْوُضُوءُ قَبْلَهُ
وَالوَضُوءُ بَعْدَهُ

"The *Barakah* of food lies in doing *Wudu* before you eat and after you finish eating."

WE HAVE LEARNED

- Allah ﷻ has given us food and drinks.
- Prophet Muhammad ﷺ said that we should do *Wudu* before and after we eat.

DO YOU KNOW THESE WORDS?
Barakah, air, breathe

Link to Workbook Lesson 24

Lesson 25 Start with *Bismillah*

TUNE IN:

بِسْمِ اللَّهِ الرَّحْمَنِ الرَّحِيمِ

In the Name Of Allah, Most Gracious, Most Merciful.
• When do we say *Bismillah*?

We should always say,
'Bismillah Ar-Rahman Ar-Rahim'
when we begin to do something.

We say it when we begin to eat our food.
We eat with our right hand.

Rasulullah ﷺ said,

سَمِّ اللَّهَ وَكُلْ بِيَمِينِكَ

"Begin with '*Bismillah*' and eat
with your right hand."

Before you eat lunch in school say '*Bismillah*'.
Before you eat dinner at home say '*Bismillah*' with your family.

WE HAVE LEARNED

- We should always say *Bismillah Ar-Rahman Ar-Rahim* when we begin to eat.
- We should try to eat with our right hand.

DO YOU KNOW THESE WORDS?
Begin, right, family, friends

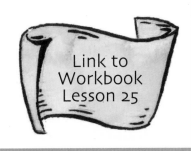

Link to Workbook Lesson 25

Lesson 26 — Drinking Water

TUNE IN:

Allah ﷻ has sent down rain as water.
We use water all the time.

• What other ways has Allah ﷻ sent us water?

Allah ﷻ has given us water to drink.
We need to drink water to live.

Some people like to drink cold water.
Some people like to drink warm water.
All of us should drink clean water.

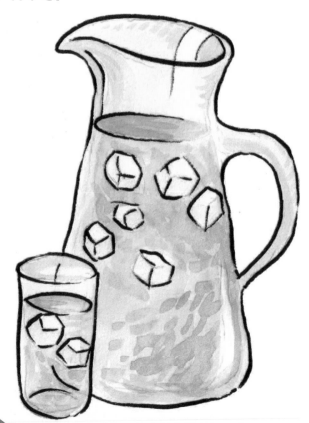

Prophet Muhammad ﷺ has said,

اِشْرَبُوا الْمَاءَ بِعُيُونِكُمْ

"Look carefully at the water before you drink it"

We get water
from rivers.

We get water
from a well.

We get water
from the sea.

We get water
from rain.

Some people throw garbage into our rivers.
They throw garbage into our oceans.

They make the water dirty.
Dirty water makes us sick.

We should keep our rivers clean.
We should keep our wells clean.
We should keep our oceans clean.
We should keep our water clean.

Let us thank Allah ﷻ for giving us water.
We must say, "*Al-Hamdulillah.*"

اَلْحَمْدُ لِلَّهِ !

WE HAVE LEARNED

- We should drink only clean water.
- We should not make the lakes, rivers and oceans dirty.
- We should thank Allah ﷻ for giving us water.

DO YOU KNOW THESE WORDS?
River, ocean, well, clean, dirty, garbage

Link to Workbook Lesson 26

Allah ﷻ made the oceans, rivers,
rain, wells, and lakes.
Allah ﷻ made water for us to drink.
We make our *Wudu* with water too.

We can drink from rivers, wells and lakes.
We cannot drink from the ocean
because it's too salty.
We should not dirty the water.
We cannot waste water.
We must save water.

List some ways we can save
water at home.

Ways to save water

1. _____
2. _____
3. _____
4. _____
5. _____
6. _____

TUNE IN:

Who is the next person after Allah ﷻ and Rasulullah ﷺ that we must love and show respect to? **Our Mother!**

One day a man came to Prophet Muhammad ﷺ. He asked, "What should I do to make Allah happy?'

Rasulullah ﷺ said, "Serve your mother."

The man said, "And then?"
Rasulullah ﷺ said, "Serve your mother."

The man said, "And then?"
Rasulullah ﷺ said,
"Serve your mother."

The man said, "And then who?"
Rasulullah ﷺ said,
"Serve your father".

أُمَّكَ، ثُمَّ أُمَّكَ، ثُمَّ أُمَّكَ، ثُمَّ أَبَاكَ.

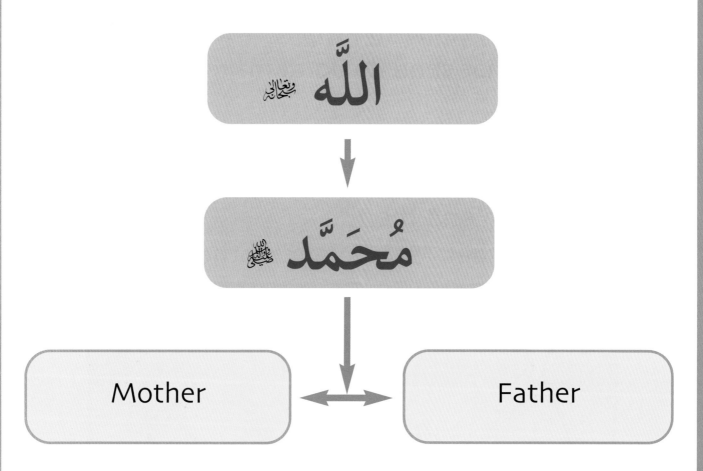

Our mothers love us.
They take care of us.
They teach us.
They are special.

I Love
You
Mother

If our mothers are happy with us,
Allah ﷾ will be happy with us.
Rasulullah ﷺ will be happy with us.

Rasulullah ﷺ said,

اِلْزَمْ رِجْلَهَا ، أَيْ أُمَّكَ ، فَثَمَّ الْجَنَّةُ

"*Jannah* lies under the feet of your mother."

WE HAVE LEARNED

- Rasulullah ﷺ taught us to care for and love our mothers.
- If our mother is happy with us, Allah ﷾ and Rasulullah ﷺ will be happy with us too.

DO YOU KNOW THESE WORDS?
Mother, teach, *Jannah*, happy

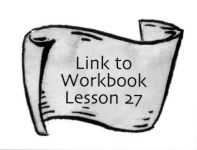

Link to
Workbook
Lesson 27

TUNE IN:

The Prophet ﷺ said: "One's faith isn't perfect till he loves for his brother what he loves for himself."

(Bukhari & Muslim)

• Have you ever received a gift?

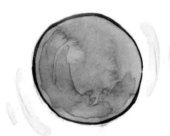

Amin and Sayid are friends.
They go to school together.
They read and play together.
They share their toys.
They share their books and lunch.

One day, Amin's mother
gave him a red ball.
He liked his red ball
very much.
He asked his mother,
"Can you get the same
ball for Sayid?"

"Why do you want the same ball for Sayid?" his mother asked.

"Because he is my friend.
I want him to have what I have."

Amin's mother loved him very much.
She got a ball for Sayid too.
They played together.

Prophet Muhammad ﷺ said,

$$\text{لاَ تُؤْمِنُوا حَتَّى تَحَابُّوا}$$

'You will not become true Muslims until you have love for each other.'"

WE HAVE LEARNED
- We should share with our friends.
- Rasulullah ﷺ told us to love each other.

DO YOU KNOW THESE WORDS?
share, love, friend, together

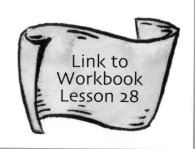

Link to
Workbook
Lesson 28

Lesson 29 — Helping Others

TUNE IN:

The Prophet ﷺ said, "Food for 1 person is enough for 2; food for 2 persons is enough for 4; food for 4 persons is enough for 8."

(Muslim)

- Do you know of anyone who feeds hungry people?

Fatima and her family like to help everyone.

Her mother helps in the soup kitchen.
She cooks lots of soup.
She gives soup to people who do not have any food.
Fatima's father drives a van every Saturday.
He takes food to sick people.
He takes the food to their homes.

Sometimes Fatima goes
with her father.
She likes to help the sick.
She likes to take care of them.

Let us share our food with the poor.
Let us share our money with the poor.
Let us share our books with the poor.
Let us do as Rasulullah ﷺ has told us to do.

WE HAVE LEARNED

- We should share our food with people who do not have any.
- We also share our money, clothes and toys.
- Prophet Muhammad ﷺ is happy with us when we share with the poor.

DO YOU KNOW THESE WORDS?
Hungry, feed, Soup Kitchen

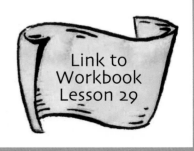

Link to
Workbook
Lesson 29

Karim and his Father

TUNE IN:

"Allah is happy with the one whose father is happy with him.
Allah is unhappy with the one whose father is unhappy with him."

(Tirmidhi, al-Hakim)

- What do you like most about your father?
  Share it with your friends.

This is Karim.
He lives with his family.
He lives with his mother.
He lives with his father.

Karim loves his father.
His father loves him too.
His father goes to school.
Karim's father is a teacher.
Karim goes with him.

Karim and his father
love to go fishing.
Karim likes to catch fish.

Karim likes to play baseball.
Karim and his father play together.

Karim and his father go to *Masjid* together.
They go to *Masjid* to pray.
They pray *Jama'ah* together.

Karim loves his father.
His father loves him.

WE HAVE LEARNED
- We should love our fathers.
- We should love our families.

DO YOU KNOW THESE WORDS?
Teacher, baseball, fishing, proud

Link to
Workbook
Lesson 30

Hadith References

For the sake of dependability we are making available the references for the Ahadith used in this book.

Page 68   "Whoever builds a masjid…." (Ahmad, al-Bukhari, Muslim, Ibn Majah, at-Tirmidhi)

Page 71   "Salah is the pillar of Islam." (at-Tabrani)

Page 74   "Pray together in Jama'ah." (an-Nisa'i)

Page 78   "Greet each other with Salam." (at-Tirmidhi)

Page 80   "Cleanliness is part of one's faith." (Muslim, Ahmad, at-Tirmidhi)

Page 82   "We should brush our teeth." (al-Bukhari)

Page 83   "Brushing your teeth makes your mouth clean and it makes Allah happy." (Ahmad, An-Nasa'i, Ibn Hibban, Ibn Majah, al-Hakim)

Page 84   "When you feel angry, keep silent." (Muslim, Ahmad)

Page 87   "The barakah of food lies in doing wudu…" (at-Tirmidhi)

Page 88   "Begin with Bismillah and eat with your right hand." (al-Bukhari, Muslim)

Page 91   "Look carefully at the water before you drink it." (Muslim)

Page 95   "Serve your mother…" (Ahmad, Abu Dawud, at-Tirmidhi, al-Hakim)

Page 98   "Jannah lies at the feet of your mother." (Muslim)

Page 100   "You will not become true Muslims until he loves…" (al-Bukhari, Muslim, at-Tirmidhi, an-Nasa'i, Ahmad, Ibn Majah)

Page 101   "Food for one person is enough for two…" (Muslim)

Page 103   "Allah is happy with the one whose father…" (At-Tirmidhi, al-Hakim)